1

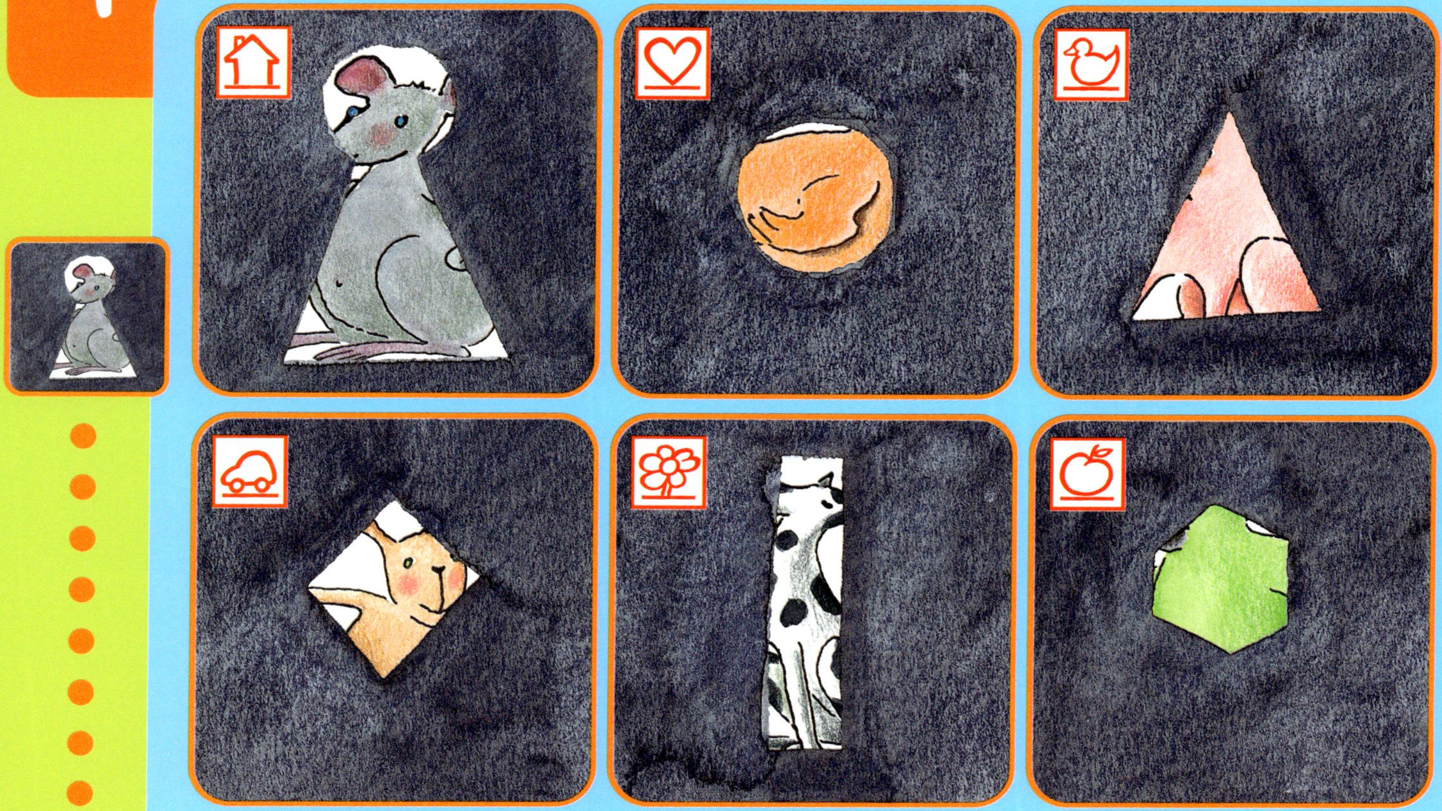

2

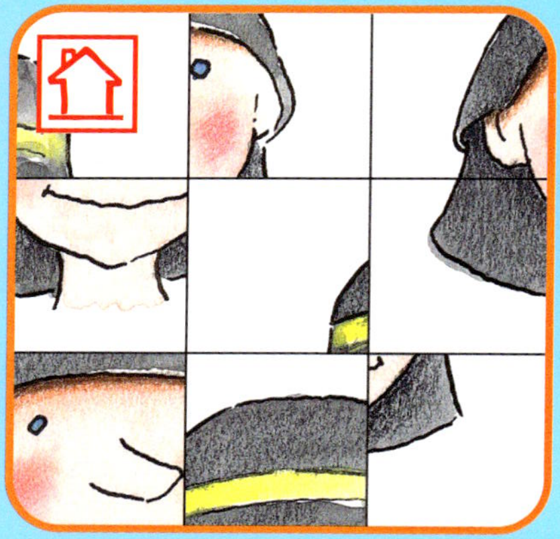

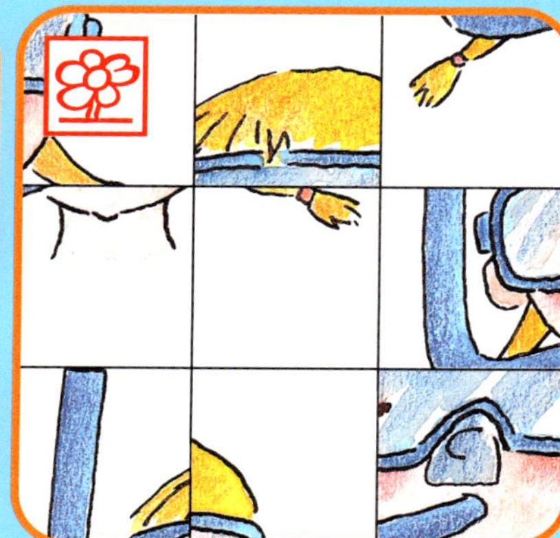

2010 2009 2008
Autor: Michael Junga
Illustrationen: Ute Ohlms, Braunschweig
Druck und Verarbeitung: westermann druck GmbH, Braunschweig
ISBN 978-3-89414-613-9

It's easy to play with bambinoLÜK:

Open the bambinoLÜK control unit und place it on the open bambino LÜK workbook. Put the six tiles symbol side up on the exercises with the same symbol, for example the tile with the red symbol 'house' on the exercise with the red symbol 'house' on the upper left hand corner.
When you have placed all the tiles on the exercises, take up the tile with the symbol 'house' and look at the exercise on which it was placed. Which picture underneath matches it? Put the tile on the matching picture. Repeat for the other five tiles and exercises. Close the bambinoLÜK control unit and turn it over. Now you can see the pattern made by the six tiles.

Everything OK?
And now have fun !

Jouer avec bambino LÜK, c'est tout simple:

Ouvre l'unité de contrôle bambino LÜK et place-la sur le cahier bambino LÜK ouvert. Place les six cartes symboles découverts sur les exercices avec les symboles correspondants, donc la carte symbole rouge «maison» sur l'exercice avec le symbole rouge «maison» en haut à gauche. Quand tu as placé les cartes, tu prends la carte symbole «maison» et tu examines l'exercice correspondant. Quelle image située en dessous correspond à cet exercice? Pose la carte sur l'image correspondante. Continue de la même façon avec les cinq cartes et exercices suivants! Puis, ferme l'unité de contrôle bambino LÜK et tourne-la vers le haut. Maintenant tu peux comparer le dessin de la solution avec celui dans le cahier.

Tout est exact ? Amuse-toi bien avec bambino LÜK !

Así jugamos con Bambino Arco:

Abre el cuaderno y coloca el estuche abierto sobre él, alineando los cuadrados del estuche con los del cuaderno. Coloca las fichas con el símbolo hacia arriba en la tapa y en la casilla del cuaderno con el mismo símbolo; por ejemplo, la ficha con el "coche" sobre el "coche" en el cuaderno. Ahora toma la ficha "casa" y mira el ejercicio en el cual estaba situada. ¿Qué dibujo se repite abajo? Coloca la ficha en la parte inferior del estuche, sobre el mismo dibujo. Repite la operación con las otras cinco fichas. Cierra el estuche y gíralo. Ahora podrás ver que se forma un dibujo, si coincide con el del libro has respondido correctamente, si no repite otra vez el proceso con las fichas equivocadas.

¡Y ahora diviértete!

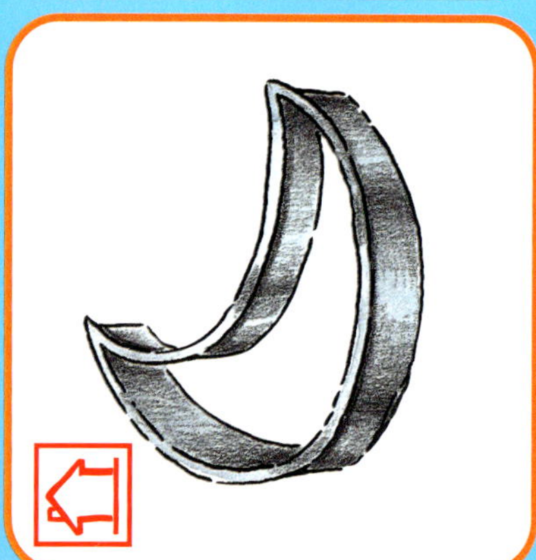

4

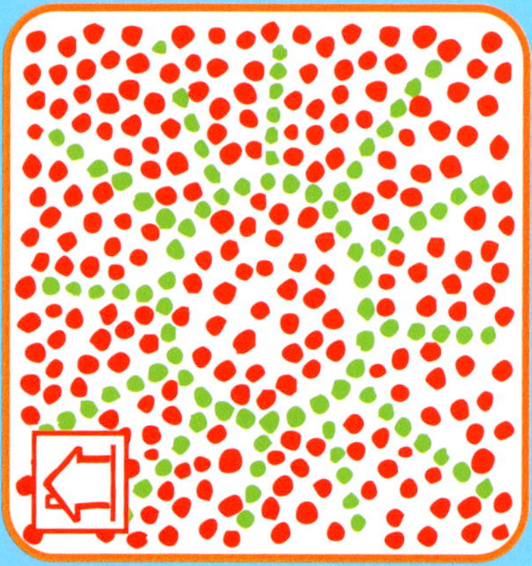
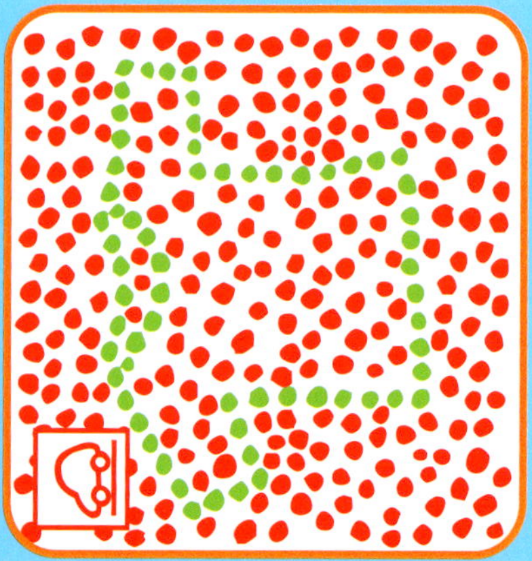

6

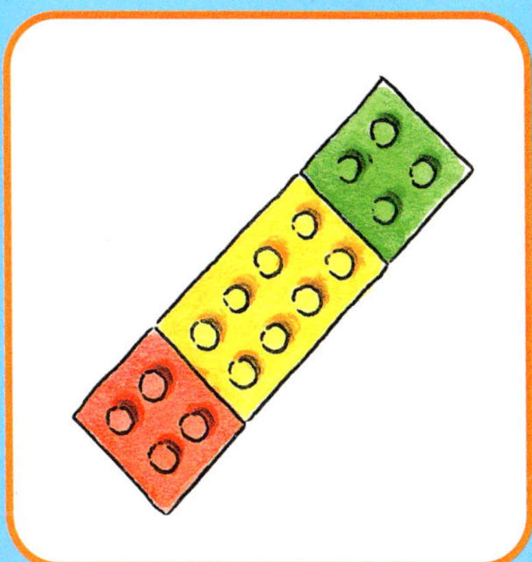
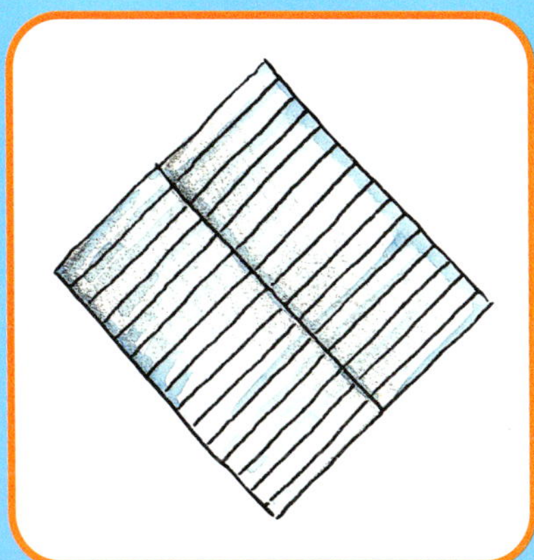

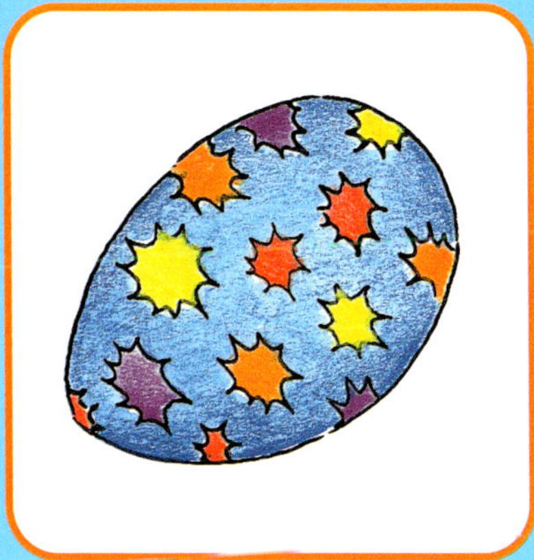

10

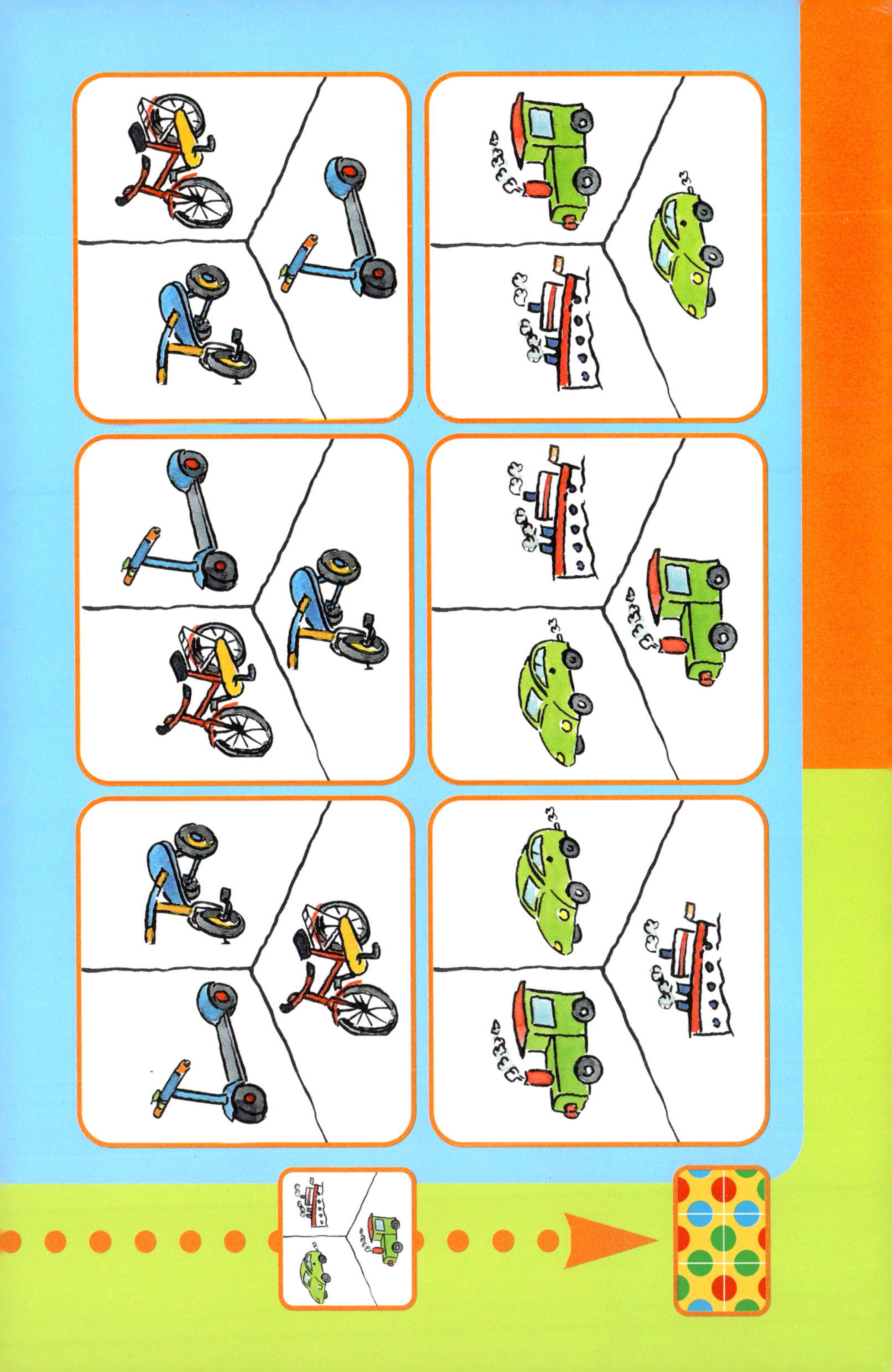

11

Inhalt Content
Table des matières Índice

1 **Was siehst du durchs Guckloch?**
2 **Gesichter zusammensetzen**
3 **Kekse backen**
4 **Tasse und Kanne**
5 **Wo ist das grüne Punktebild?**
6 **Wie sieht das von oben aus?**
7 **Wo ist das gleiche Ei?**
8 **Was wird daraus gestrickt?**
9 **Wo ist der gleiche Fisch?**
10 **Suche das Gleiche!**
11 **Lückenpuzzle**

Die Kinder müssen genau beobachten, vergleichen und zuordnen können, wenn sie die Übungen fehlerfrei lösen wollen. Durch diese aufmerksame Mitarbeit wird ihre allgemeine Konzentrationsfähigkeit nachhaltig gestärkt und weiterentwickelt.

1 **What can you see through the spyhole?**
2 **Putting together faces**
3 **Making biscuits**
4 **Cup and coffee pot**
5 **Where is the green dotted picture?**
6 **What does it look like from above?**
7 **Where is the same egg?**
8 **What do you knit from that?**
9 **Where is the same fish?**
10 **Look for the same thing!**
11 **Puzzle with missing pieces**

The children need to observe, compare and relate accurately in order to complete the exercises without mistakes. By focussing on their work their general ability to concentrate will be strengthened and developed.